The New York Times

CALM AND BREEZY MINI CROSSWORDS

The New York Times

CALM AND BREEZY MINI CROSSWORDS
150 Easy Fun-Sized Puzzles

Joel Fagliano

ST. MARTIN'S GRIFFIN
NEW YORK

First published in the United States by St. Martin's Griffin,
an imprint of St. Martin's Publishing Group

www.stmartins.com

ISBN 978-1-250-79795-7

Our books may be purchased in bulk for promotional, educational, or
business use. Please contact your local bookseller or the Macmillan Corporate
and Premium Sales Department at 1-800-221-7945, extension 5442, or by email at
MacmillanSpecialMarkets@macmillan.com.

First Edition: 2021

11   10   9   8   7   6

The New York Times

CALM AND BREEZY MINI CROSSWORDS

Introduction

When you think about it, crosswords are particularly well-suited for our fast-paced, modern age. Almost every clue and answer is on a different subject, your mind bounces from one thing to the next, and when a puzzle's not too hard, it takes only a short time to do.

Well, if regular crosswords are modern, *The New York Times*'s new Mini crosswords are hypermodern. The clues and answers are just as diverse, but each 5×5-square grid takes a mere minute or so to complete—even less once you get good. You now feel the rush of excitement in finishing a puzzle in a fraction of the time!

Launched in 2014, and originally available only digitally, the Mini has become so popular that now on weekdays it also appears in print in the main section of the paper.

Each Mini is created by Joel Fagliano, the paper's digital crosswords editor, who started selling regular crosswords to the *Times* when he was seventeen. To date he's had more than 50 weekday and Sunday crosswords published in the paper, becoming in the process one of the most popular and accomplished puzzlemakers.

Joel packs his Minis with lively vocabulary, modern references, and the sort of playfulness and intelligence you'll find in its big brother elsewhere in the paper. The Minis are easy/medium in difficulty. The cultural references skew young. But don't let the small size and big squares fool you. These puzzles are decidedly for adults.

On the following pages are 150 Minis from the *Times,* lightly re-edited for their first publication in book form.

Let the many rushes of excitement begin!

—Will Shortz

ACROSS

1 Transportation option
4 Taken ___ (surprised)
7 Back in style
8 Transportation option
9 Org. into which Ben Simmons was drafted first in 2016

DOWN

1 Transportation option in S.F.
2 Modern transportation option
3 The devil
5 Baby's bed
6 Hawaiian coffee region

1	2	3		
4			5	6
7				
8				
		9		

ACROSS

1 "Monsters, ___" (Pixar film)
4 9 a.m. to 5 p.m., commonly
7 Satellite's path
8 Unit of a sushi roll
9 Morning dampness

DOWN

1 Restaurant that offers Rooty-Tooty Fresh 'N Fruity Pancakes
2 Edible seaweed used as a sushi wrap
3 To the third power
5 Sushi ingredient
6 Dish prepared in a Crock-Pot

	1	2	3	4
5				
6				
7				
8				

ACROSS

1 ___ Punk ("Get Lucky" band)
5 Dessert with a hyphen in its name
6 Aggressive Texas Hold 'Em bet
7 Ebony's partner, in song
8 Intersection of amphibians and Republican politics

DOWN

1 Investigate, with "into"
2 Permit
3 Smile from across the bar, say
4 Broadway award
5 Indian believer in nonviolence to all living creatures

4

ACROSS

1 Many a Parisian hangout for Hemingway
5 Base's counterpart
6 Expensively stylish
7 Physician who once appeared regularly with Oprah
8 ___ Pictures ("Spider-Man" studio)

DOWN

1 Where Tahrir Square is located
2 Follow, as advice
3 Like soda after shaking
4 Big name in ice cream
6 Avenues and streets: Abbr.

ACROSS

1 Word following bachelor or scratch
4 Shoe bottoms
6 Country between Chile and Brazil
8 Bringing together
9 "See ya!"
10 Serious grime
11 Bee follower

DOWN

1 Body ___ (all the people in a country)
2 The tiniest bit
3 Break from the norm
4 Dusty Springfield's "___ a Preacher Man"
5 Golfer Vijay who's won three majors
6 Reason for an app crash
7 In the past

6

	1	2	3	4
5				
6				
7				
8				

ACROSS
1 Twitter ___
5 Matriarch of the Weasley family, in the "Harry Potter" books
6 Wedding party?
7 Participated in a play
8 Oracle

DOWN
1 The "F" in the equation "F = ma"
2 1% group
3 Esteemed member of a tribe
4 Colored, as hair
5 Degrees for Mitt Romney and Michael Bloomberg

	1	2	3	4	5
6					
7					
8					

ACROSS

1 Storage for fast web page retrieval
6 Coiner of the phrase "15 minutes of fame"
7 Inbox buildup
8 Election year event

DOWN

1 Showed up
2 Part of U.A.E.
3 ____ Pet (sprouting figure)
4 Lester ____, moderator for a 2016 8-Across
5 Alternatively
6 Marry

8

¹	²	³	⁴	■
⁵				⁶
⁷				
⁸				
■	⁹			

ACROSS

1 Triple Crown component in baseball
5 Coffee additive
7 Luxurious country house
8 Flop down wearily, from Yiddish
9 Amount of medicine to take

DOWN

1 "Let us know if you're coming" initials
2 Put up, as a house
3 Snow-block house
4 Smelling ——
6 Knock down, as a house

9

1	2	3	4	5
6				
7				
8				
9				

ACROSS

1 Group that you might be eager to have as party guests
6 "The Divine Comedy" writer
7 Revealed to be gay
8 It's avoided on a gluten-free diet
9 Like an eager party guest

DOWN

1 Maker of Acrobat and Photoshop
2 First lady before Michelle
3 ___ Milan (Italian soccer powerhouse)
4 Total bargain
5 Stuffed bear

	1	2	3	4
5				
6				
7				
8				

ACROSS

1 "S" on a shaker
5 Prefix with -graph on an old copier
6 American abroad, e.g.
7 Jobs who co-founded Apple
8 Jekyll's counterpart

DOWN

1 Common highway speed
2 Extremely excited
3 Winning side in the Brexit vote
4 Classic NPR fundraising giveaway
5 Go well together

1	2	3	■	■
4			5	6
7				
8				
■		9		

ACROSS

1 Many a craft brew
4 Protesting N.F.L. QB Kaepernick
7 It makes the cut
8 Ingredient in bread and beer making
9 Signal from a sinking ship

DOWN

1 Totally gross
2 Type of corn bread
3 Assumed name
5 "Should that be the case . . ."
6 Keeps after taxes

ACROSS

1 Bezos who founded Amazon
5 Person transporting a mattress, maybe
6 Hawaiian "thank you"
7 Fried food said to have been invented at the Texas State Fair
8 Out of bed
9 House for a lord
10 Truman's Marshall

DOWN

1 Second-most common U.S. surname, after Smith
2 One avoiding paying taxes, e.g.
3 Serious criminal
4 Butterfly : caterpillar :: ___ : pollywog
5 Yacht's docking spot
6 "Idleness brings want," for Aesop's "The Ants and the Grasshopper"
7 Sleep in a tent

	1	2	3	
4				5
6				
7				
	8			

ACROSS

1 Insult
4 Popular payment app
6 Following behind, as a trailer
7 Your brother's daughter, to you
8 Rev. who said "We must rise to the majestic heights of meeting physical force with soul force"

DOWN

1 It's in your jeans
2 Seller of nonedible chips
3 Artist's garment
4 Coq au ___
5 Need to pay

14

	1	2	3	4
5				
6				
7				
8				

ACROSS
1 Side that the British drive on
5 Polish person?
6 Indian currency
7 Have ___ to play
8 Get a grade above F

DOWN
1 Conservative pundit Ingraham
2 Montreal team that became the Washington Nationals
3 Right in the ___ (deeply affecting, in modern slang)
4 Spruce or sycamore
5 Sandwich in a tortilla

1	2	3	4	
5				6
7				
8				
9				

ACROSS

1 Tackle behind the line of scrimmage
5 Skydiver's jumping-off point
7 After, in French
8 Baby otter or dog
9 Downright mean

DOWN

1 What salmon do upriver
2 ___ Centauri (closest star system to ours)
3 Gives a darn
4 Was in the front row of a team photo, say
6 Catch sight of

16

	1	2	3	4
5				
6				
7				
8				

ACROSS

1 Sign on a door
5 Democrats or Republicans
6 Michael Jackson's "Thriller," e.g.
7 Country singer Rimes
8 Michael Jackson's "Thriller," e.g.

DOWN

1 Diet that excludes processed foods, informally
2 ___ Outfitters (clothing store)
3 Attacked by a bee
4 "The Battle ___ of the Republic"
5 Buddies

ACROSS

1 "___ is the measure of all things": Protagoras
4 Prominent surrogate campaigner for Clinton in 2016
7 Banana Republic rival
8 DiCaprio won his first in 2016
9 Cunning

DOWN

1 Self-confidence
2 They can be sung to the tune of "Twinkle, Twinkle, Little Star"
3 Agents making drug busts
5 Lunch or dinner
6 Out of kilter

18

1	2	3	4	5
6				
7				
8				
9				

ACROSS
1 Chinese zodiac reptile
6 Feature of sales in Delaware and Oregon
7 Top floor of a house
8 Answer to the riddle "I have keys but no locks and feet but no socks, what am I?"
9 Throat ailment

DOWN
1 Sounds made with the thumb and middle finger
2 Untagged, in a game of tag
3 Perfume from rose petals
4 2016 debater with Pence
5 Former member of the force

19

ACROSS

1 Agreement between governments
5 ___ Minh City, Vietnam
6 Bird on a Froot Loops box
7 What T.S.A. requires along with your boarding pass
8 Monet or Manet, par exemple
9 Type again, as a password
10 Mother who was canonized in 2016

DOWN

1 Canadian dish of French fries topped with cheese and gravy
2 Loudly confronts
3 Spiced brew
4 "Swipe right" dating app
5 Owl, when it calls
6 Steph Curry's signature basketball shot
7 Divide, as the Red Sea

20

	1	2	3	
4	○	○	○	5
6			○	
7			○	
8			○	

ACROSS

1 Volcanic spew
4 Pet peeves?
6 Popular pain reliever
7 Crust, mantle or outer core
8 ___ apso (dog breed)

DOWN

1 To whom Muslims pray
2 "I'm out of here"
3 Privileged people
4 Season with color changes, as represented literally by the circled letters
5 Word that fills both blanks of "Que ___, ___"

21

1	2	3	4	5
6				
7				
8				
9				■

ACROSS
1 Hard-to-find guy in a crowd
6 Killer whales
7 Social ___
8 Contest submission
9 Dark blue shade

DOWN
1 Bathroom door sign
2 Basketball venue
3 Samsung purchase (warning: no vowels)
4 What the lactose intolerant avoid
5 "___, can you see . . ."

22

	1	2	3	4
5				
6				
7				
8				

ACROSS

1 Mediterranean and Caribbean
5 Capital of Afghanistan
6 Symbol seen in a smartphone text
7 Hit the town
8 ____ Fifth Avenue

DOWN

1 American ____, territory in the South Pacific
2 Kindle purchase
3 How roast beef may be served
4 Thin cut
5 Barrels of beer

1	2	3		
4			5	6
7				
8				
		9		

ACROSS

1 A.T.M. fig. that's an anagram of A.T.M.
4 Get to
7 Word before powder or Pebbles
8 Does the breaststroke or butterfly
9 "If I'm being truthful," in text messages

DOWN

1 Paths for basketball shots
2 Catty comment?
3 Unspoken, but implied
5 Hair parter
6 ___ browns (breakfast side)

24

ACROSS

1 With 3-Across, soup veggies, represented literally
3 "___ I was saying . . ."
5 Vision-correcting procedure
7 Company that made Pong and Asteroids
8 Relinquished
9 With 10-Across, hair problem, represented literally
10 Grades from 65–69

DOWN

1 TV's Melrose ___
2 Gobbled up
3 Put on television
4 Loses control on an icy road
6 Feeling blue

ACROSS

1 Vehicle not known for its m.p.g. efficiency
4 Jam band with a Ben & Jerry's flavor named for them
7 Major artery
8 "___ of the Dead" (2004 zombie movie send-up)
9 There are 2,000 in a ton: Abbr.

DOWN

1 Places for cucumber facials
2 "Houston, we have a problem . . ."
3 Shared widely on social media
5 Result of a split ticket?
6 ___ Christian Andersen

26

ACROSS

1 Defamation in print
6 Apple application that stores music
8 Beer brewed in upstate New York
10 "Open, sesame!" speaker
11 One looking up restaurant reviews on their phone, say
12 John ___ (tractor maker)

DOWN

1 Bart's sister on "The Simpsons"
2 Country with a red, white and green flag
3 Hid, as a squirrel might an acorn
4 Allow
5 Delaware tribe
7 ___-toothed tiger
9 Suffix with Obama

ACROSS

1 24 bottles of beer, e.g.
5 Nuts and ___
6 Victorious
7 Female reproductive organ
8 Fashion prefix with -core

DOWN

1 Discussion, slangily
2 Where vows are exchanged at a wedding
3 Hurricane, e.g.
4 Catch sight of
5 Huge benefit

28

1	2	3	4	5
6				
7				
8				
	9			

ACROSS

1 Intense passion
6 Tired
7 Upper crust of society
8 Some Surrealist paintings
9 End string of the alphabet

DOWN

1 Filled with wonder
2 "I have this totally under control"
3 "The ___ Show," vehicle for Trevor Noah
4 Red Sox great David
5 Deli loaves

ACROSS

1 Driving test?
5 Liquefying blender setting
6 Parkwood Entertainment, for Beyoncé
7 Throw out, as a tenant
8 Shower alternative

DOWN

1 Tropical fruit with pink pulp
2 Planet's path
3 Bloodsucking worm
4 Pool table cloth
5 Commoner

30

¹	²	³	⁴	■
⁵				■
⁶			⁷	
⁸				
■	⁹			

ACROSS

1 "___, poor Yorick!": Hamlet
5 Scrabble piece
6 See 2-Down
8 See 2-Down
9 Kanga's little one, in "Winnie-the-Pooh"

DOWN

1 Not much
2 With 6- and 8-Across, shared belief of Christianity and Islam
3 ___ boy (priest's assistant)
4 Take care of
7 Greek letter between pi and sigma

1	2	3	4	
5				
6				7
	8			
	9			

ACROSS

1 Step on a ladder
5 French friend
6 Commerce pact discussed in the 2016 presidential debates
8 Recipe direction
9 Lip-____ (pretend to sing)

DOWN

1 Participated in a marathon
2 Amherst school, informally
3 Pretty cool
4 Be accepted to, as a college
7 Curved path

32

ACROSS

1 Sch. where "Good Will Hunting" is set
4 Animal with distinctive stripes
6 Expression that doesn't translate literally
7 Gadget
8 Pen cover

DOWN

1 Doctor
2 Spanish island known for its party scene
3 Walk around loudly
4 Sharp turn
5 "Yo te ____," Spanish for "I love you"

ACROSS

1 "Cut me some ____!"
6 Cleveland Cavalier's superstar, to fans
7 Automaker that created the 911
8 Sound blaster at a concert
9 ____-haw
10 Part of a pool with a diving board
12 Those under 18, legally
13 ____ level position

DOWN

1 Satan's disguise in the Garden of Eden
2 Weight abbr.
3 Sportsman's reason to take a bow?
4 Songwriter Leonard and Times columnist Roger
5 Attacked M.M.A-style
6 Chinese noodle dish
7 Anakin's love in "Star Wars"
11 "____ favor" (Spanish "please")

34

1	2	3	4	5
6				
7				
8				
9				■

ACROSS
1 Newscaster Wallace
6 G.P.S. offering
7 "Shoot!"
8 "___ you so!"
9 Like some horror films

DOWN
1 Daniel who plays James Bond
2 Genre of instructional YouTube videos
3 Something heard on the grapevine
4 Boot-shaped country
5 Texter's button

ACROSS

1 Subj. that covers atoms and elements
5 Site for streaming TV
6 Cars at Hollywood premieres
7 How contracts are usually signed
8 Word after lily and launching

DOWN

1 Home to 1.3+ billion people
2 Like rainforest air, usually
3 With 4-Down, SpaceX founder
4 See 3-Down
6 Where Burt's Bees or Blistex is applied

36

1	2	3	4	5
6				
7				
8				
9				

ACROSS

1 Gate fastener
6 "Howdy," in Maui
7 Falafel holders
8 Turn away, as one's gaze
9 Tart and flavorful

DOWN

1 Bolivian capital
2 ___ and kicking
3 "Definitely," in slang
4 Excel creation
5 Quick and not well-thought-out

	1	2	3	4
5				
6				
7				
8				

ACROSS

1 Pinnacle
5 To a great extent, in a 2016 coinage
6 Halo wearer
7 Apple ___ (site of a Genius Bar)
8 "Critique of Pure Reason" philosopher

DOWN

1 One of Columbus's ships
2 Goad
3 Tip off
4 "South Park" kid
5 Lounge in the sun

38

ACROSS

1 Building access feature for the disabled
5 One point from a service break, in tennis
7 Magna ___
8 One might end "Sent from my iPhone"
9 Harmonize

DOWN

1 What horses and hearts can do
2 John Quincy ___
3 Kind of eel
4 Russia's president
6 Soft mineral

ACROSS

1 Physician with a daily talk show
5 E, I, E, I or O
7 Big name in surround sound
8 Howard of satellite radio
9 Record label for Otis Redding

DOWN

1 VHS tape displacers
2 With "the," Jimmy Fallon's house band
3 Baby bird of prey
4 Lion's prey
6 Wildcat with tufted ears

40

ACROSS

1 Boyfriends
6 Jack-o'-lantern material
8 Ethiopia's neighbor on the Horn of Africa
9 Fix, as an election
10 .300 is a good one in baseball: Abbr.
11 Transports to Staten Island
13 College officials
14 Miss identification

DOWN

1 ___ the lede (wasn't forthright)
2 Political refugees
3 Appropriate
4 From whom Russia annexed the Crimean Peninsula
5 Chef's strainers
6 Ideal, in teen slang
7 Hounds or badgers
12 "Go, team, go!"

	1	2	3	4
5				
6				
7				
8				

ACROSS

1 Candle blower's thought
5 ___ Wonka
6 Fastest-growing religion in the world
7 Talk show host Kelly
8 Opposite of cons

DOWN

1 Older but ___
2 Response to "Any volunteers?"
3 Is outstanding, in modern slang
4 "What a Friend We Have in Jesus," for one
5 Chicken (out)

42

ACROSS

1 Move like a bunny
4 Say "Boo!" to
6 See 1-Down
7 "Ripley's Believe It ___!"
8 Explosive compound

DOWN

1 What a ghost may do to a 6-Across
2 Approximately
3 Amanda of "Togetherness"
4 Bar order with a chaser
5 Candy ___

ACROSS

1 Easy as ___
4 "Get outta here!"
6 180° reversal
7 "Beats me"
8 Easy as ___

DOWN

1 Malfunction (or an important AIDS advocacy group)
2 Times op-ed columnist Frank
3 Mexican meat
4 French for "south"
5 Letters on the "6" button

44

	1	2	3	4
	5			
6				
7				■
8				■

ACROSS

1 "Man, that was a close call!"
5 ___ Abedin, top Clinton aide
6 Boo-boo kisser
7 Clever strategy
8 His and ___

DOWN

1 Alternative to skim, 1% and 2%
2 It's good for a laugh
3 Annual awards presented in Los Angeles
4 Route
6 Speed limit abbr.

ACROSS
1 "C" on a faucet
5 Cabs ordered from an app
7 Lacking skill in
8 Chimney output
9 All over again

DOWN
1 2016 World Series team
2 Famous resident of Chicago's South Side
3 Deceived
4 Rapper whose real name is Aubrey Graham
6 Crockpot dish

46

ACROSS

1 Airport in Queens
4 Rock layer accessed in fracking
6 See 1-Down
7 David Brooks pieces
8 "___ the season . . ."

DOWN

1 With 6-Across, F.B.I. director during the 2016 election
2 Hightailed it out of town
3 Delete and Return, e.g.
4 Kilt wearer
5 Arizona tribe

47

ACROSS

1 Backstage guest
4 Outpatient treatment centers
8 Like some bars with a view
9 Feel sick
10 ___-pitch softball
11 Vince Gilligan, vis-à-vis "Breaking Bad"
13 Popular Halloween costume with a red sweater and moustache
14 Faucet

DOWN

1 Word that fills the Shakespeare quote, "These ___ delights have ___ ends"
2 Like Beethoven's Sixth Symphony, keywise
3 Service break during the Indy 500
4 Notable feature of the Liberty Bell
5 Longest river in France
6 Punctuation mark that makes eyes in an emoticon
7 Reproductive part of a fungus
12 Lawyer's org.

48

1	2	3	4	
5				6
7				
8				
	9			

ACROSS

1 Home to Des Moines
5 Game with tiny bats and a stand
7 Hairlike propellers of protozoans
8 Keller who was portrayed in "The Miracle Worker"
9 Ship

DOWN

1 Poison ivy symptom
2 New York theater awards
3 Pixar robot
4 One who's not from around here?
6 Hit the tarmac

49

49

1	2	3	4	5
6				
7				
8				
9				

ACROSS

1 Ice cream covering at a Japanese restaurant
6 Felt sore
7 Crystal-filled rock
8 Japanese comics style
9 Heavenly harp player

DOWN

1 Molten rock
2 Majority of a world map
3 Cheech and ___
4 Row of bushes
5 "In an ___ world . . ."

50

ACROSS
1 Participate in a democracy
5 Election ____
6 U.S. citizenship island
7 Mournful poem
8 Dot's Morse code counterpart

DOWN
1 Luxurious country estate
2 Leers at lecherously
3 Certain chicken piece
4 Online place to buy homemade crafts
5 On a ____-to-know basis

ACROSS

1 Instrument on Guinness bottles
5 Instrument similar to the bassoon
6 Instrument that comes in a kit
7 Beginning
8 Opposite of WNW

DOWN

1 "French" and "English" instruments
2 Bad treatment
3 It wasn't built in a day
4 Pain in the neck
6 Female deer

ACROSS

1 Rite ___ (drugstore)
4 Overthrow attempts
7 Alternative to a Facebook status or Instagram post
8 Dance that's also a dip
9 Word before milk or beans

DOWN

1 Parts of a play
2 Presidential caucus state
3 Battles like Hamilton vs. Burr
5 Mexican currency
6 Stick around

ACROSS

1 Word in several U.S. state names
4 Chocolate substitute
6 Nickname for Barack Obama
7 Result on the SAT
8 Ask nosy questions

DOWN

1 Anti-racism grp. since 1909
2 Miscue
3 Stevie Wonder's "Don't You ___ 'bout a Thing"
4 "The Big Bang Theory" airer
5 "See ya!"

54

ACROSS

1 Bedtime clothes, briefly
4 Sporty Mazda model
6 Industry for Wells Fargo and Chase
8 One-named star with the 2016 #1 album "Anti"
9 Drinker's potbelly
10 $15/hour and the like
11 ___ es Salaam

DOWN

1 Fool . . . or the villain in "Hellraiser"
2 Indonesia's capital of 14+ million
3 End of a scorpion's tail
4 Street photographer Vivian ___
5 Year: Latin
6 "Wait one sec," in text message shorthand
7 Slangy term for a pistol

ACROSS

1 Tall story
5 Not liquid or gas
6 Rubber-stamping
7 Cry of dismay
8 Sock fillers

DOWN

1 2020 Olympics host
2 Dead or ___
3 Election day annoyances
4 Like much of Bill Maher's comedy
5 Chimney build-up

56

ACROSS
1 Charleston ____ (candy)
5 Nun's attire
7 Fragile atmospheric layer
8 Vice president after Biden
9 Caustic cleaning solutions

DOWN
1 Word after karate or pork
2 Brownish-green eye color
3 Black piano key material
4 React to a really bad pun
6 Golfer's pegs

	1	2	3	4
5				
6				
7				
8				

ACROSS

1 N.B.A. honorees, briefly
5 Like the New York Times mini puzzle
6 Cook's cover-up in the kitchen
7 "Magic" instrument in a Mozart title
8 ___ Ocean, Julia Roberts's "Ocean's Eleven" role

DOWN

1 ___ syrup
2 Flu cause
3 Story lines
4 "Auld Lang ___"
5 Crazy

58

ACROSS
1 University aides, for short
4 Civil War side, with "the"
6 Home to the Taj Mahal
7 Result of turning heads?
8 Animal that sleeps upside down

DOWN
1 Like the Chinese and Thai languages
2 The "A" in A/V
3 Circus height enhancer
4 Plops down in a chair
5 Make a ___ of (bungle)

ACROSS

1 Hannibal famously crossed them with elephants
5 "Get away, fly!"
6 They're used for snowmen's eyes
7 Latin for 8-Across
8 Animal on California's flag

DOWN

1 Stick out like ___ thumb
2 ___ apso (dog breed)
3 Kind of 8-Across in Coca-Cola ads
4 Distress call letters
6 Baby 8-Across

60

1	2	3	4	5
6				
7				
8				
9				

ACROSS

1 Mine passage
6 Military training group
7 For two, in French
8 Brought back to life, as a candle
9 Ridges on a guitar's neck

DOWN

1 Winter neckwear
2 Bill who played Stefon on "S.N.L."
3 "Hello" singer, 2015
4 Apple, but not a PC
5 Messages with emojis

ACROSS

1 Important exam for college applicants
4 Sales slip: Abbr.
7 First, in Spanish
9 Containing many things, as a Congressional spending bill
10 Makes fun of
11 Contaminates
13 More intensely passionate
14 "Wahoo!"
15 YouTube video lead-ins

DOWN

1 Apple Music alternative
2 Country between Turkey and Azerbaijan
3 "30 Rock" creator
4 1940 Hitchcock film that won Best Picture
5 Having a hard outer layer
6 Talking-____ (scoldings)
8 Cheapskate
12 Jrs. one year later

62

ACROSS

1 Four of the 12 Imams of Shia Islam
5 Designer Chanel
6 Refused to budge from one's position
7 Country in a 2015 nuclear deal
8 Yin and ___

DOWN

1 Automaker with the ILX, RLX and TLX
2 Boston airport
3 Cake covering
4 Male offspring
6 Built without professional help, for short

The grid:

1	2	3	4	■
5				6
7				
8				
■	9			

ACROSS

1 Watch chains
5 Foul-smelling
7 Reeves in many Internet memes
8 Having a roof overhang
9 See 1-Down

DOWN

1 With 9-Across, bogus stories on Facebook, for example
2 Pacific or Indian
3 Courageous
4 Bone-muscle connector
6 Clothing, slangily

64

1	2	3	4	5
6				
7				
8				
9				

ACROSS

1 Capital of Senegal
6 Put pen to paper
7 Senate staffers
8 Diameter halves
9 Errol ____, star of "Captain Blood"

DOWN

1 ____ planet (what Pluto is)
2 Built-in Windows font
3 ____ pool (inflatable backyard toy)
4 Didn't go out for dinner
5 Sticky substance exuded by pine trees

1	2	3	4	5
6				
7				
8				
■	9			

ACROSS

1 Lizard known to lick its own eyeballs
6 One-time surgery anesthetic
7 Gleamed
8 Godzilla's stomping ground
9 Caribbean and Baltic

DOWN

1 Heroic exploit
2 Cultural value system
3 Fail in the clutch
4 Its capital is Nairobi
5 Crumbled cookies in "dirt pudding"

66

	1	2	3	4
	5			
6				
7				■
8				■

ACROSS

1 School in the Bay Area, for short
5 Turkey club?
6 Number of strikes in a turkey, in bowling
7 Seedy bar
8 Drove 100 m.p.h., e.g.

DOWN

1 Not cool
2 Perform a turkey task
3 Knight's horse
4 Enemy
6 N.F.L. six-pointers: Abbr.

	1	2	3	4
	5			
6				
7				
8				

ACROSS

1 "Mamma Mia!" group
5 Major-leaguers
6 Piece of Thanksgiving leftovers
7 Piece of Thanksgiving leftovers
8 Poems of praise

DOWN

1 Ladybug's prey
2 It gets into a pickle
3 Wade ____, Hall-of-Famer with 3,010 hits
4 Cigarette's end
6 Number under @ on a keyboard

ACROSS

1 Toys for snow days
6 ___ Tomatoes
7 Chipotle offering
8 "The Walking Dead" channel
9 Dove's sound
10 "I can't hear you!"
12 The "T" of TBS
13 Up to now

DOWN

1 Witchcraft
2 U.S.P.S. delivery: Abbr.
3 Boarding pass on one's phone
4 Frustrating road sign
5 "Tha Doggfather" rapper, to fans
6 Commotion
7 "Enough!," in Italy
11 Suffix with meth- or hex-

1	2	3	4	5
6				
7				
8				
9				

ACROSS

1 Hanging ___ (issues in the 2000 election)
6 Violin bow application
7 Publicist's concern
8 Word before circus or bias
9 Putting a rubber snake in someone's bed, e.g.

DOWN

1 Pinch, as a piecrust
2 "Odyssey" author
3 Carne ___
4 "Go ahead, start eating!"
5 Move furtively

ACROSS

1 Docs prescribe them
5 Eldest Baldwin brother
6 What has a bed but never sleeps, a mouth but never eats?
8 Fan's publication
9 ___ and Ani (jewelry giant)

DOWN

1 Disfigure
2 ___ Doolittle, "My Fair Lady" lady
3 Beelzebub
4 Part of "CSI"
7 "Oedipus ___"

ACROSS

1 Pop music's Lady ___
5 Capital of South Korea
6 It's just over a foot
7 Casino dice game
8 Typists tap them

DOWN

1 Netflix category
2 Totally fine
3 Nervous swallows
4 They have hops and heads
5 Hit the ___ (sleep)

72

¹	²	³	⁴	
⁵				⁶
⁷				
⁸				
⁹				

ACROSS

1 Fit and muscular
5 Birdlike
7 Florida senator Marco
8 Kagan of the Supreme Court
9 ___ Vader

DOWN

1 Exposed, as teeth
2 Dangler in the back of one's throat
3 Substance in a bran muffin
4 Barely audible
6 He put two and two together in the Bible

	1	2	3	4
5				
6				
7				
8				

ACROSS

1 Worm on a hook, e.g.
5 Perceive
6 Bird in the Anheuser-Busch logo
7 Disney film set in ancient China
8 Checkout line count

DOWN

1 Fine example of something, slangily
2 Each one in a square is 90°
3 Its founder was born in Mecca
4 Much of the Disney Channel's demographic
5 Game before a final

74

	1	2	3	4
■	5			
6				
7				■
8				■

ACROSS

1 "____ right up . . ."
5 Black-and-white religious figures
6 Black-and-white animal
7 Black-and-white cookie
8 Seabird with a forked tail

DOWN

1 Part of a drum kit
2 One doing piano repair
3 Close with
4 Free TV ad, for short
6 One calling the kettle black, in a saying

ACROSS

1 "I say, old ___!"
5 Give a hard time
8 Gum brand available in "Fire" and "Ice"
9 Colored like ketchup
10 Sprinted
11 PC outlet
13 Snoopy's dog breed
14 Guys and ___

DOWN

1 Ricotta or romano
2 Pocketbook
3 The "A" in MoMA
4 Big expense for an employer
6 Catches the game?
7 Emailed
8 Defeat soundly
12 Org. with lots of clubs

ACROSS

1 Go "ptui!"
5 Greasy
6 Feeling lightheaded and silly
8 Eye part containing the iris
9 Sewing line

DOWN

1 Pine-___
2 Very devout
3 "___ Lucy" (classic sitcom)
4 Perfectionist, personality-wise
7 Vegetable that's a month backwards

1	2	3	4	5
6				
7				
8				
9				

ACROSS

1 Mixes with a spoon
6 Tiny parasites
7 "Let me restate that . . ."
8 Office fill-ins
9 Letter after "ar"

DOWN

1 Strike down (anagram of 6-Across)
2 New York ____ (anagram of 6-Across)
3 List entries (anagram of 6-Across)
4 Gather, as grain
5 Taxpayer IDs: Abbr.

ACROSS

1 Reaction to an Internet meme, maybe
4 Outlying community
7 Spooky
8 Swiss Army ___
9 ___ Spiegel (German magazine)

DOWN

1 Onion relative used in soups
2 Pair pulling a plow
3 Sensationalist, as a tabloid headline
5 Teeming (with)
6 Case load?

ACROSS

1 Be effusive with one's praise
5 It's around a yard
6 Group of teachers or teamsters
7 "___ Andronicus" (Shakespeare play)
8 Spiciness, or another name for a lemon peel

DOWN

1 "Three wishes" granter
2 Meters and liters, e.g.
3 Often-sacrificed piece in the game Stratego
4 Roosters' mates
5 Fiddle around (with)

80

ACROSS

1 President Bartlet of "The West Wing"
4 When doubled, comforting words
6 Camel's watering hole
7 Ford F-150, e.g.
8 Authorizes

DOWN

1 His birthdate anchors our calendars
2 One of the Trumps
3 Post-monologue spot for Stephen Colbert
4 Dorothy's dog
5 "___! The Herald Angels Sing"

	1	2	3	
4				5
6				
7				
	8			

ACROSS

1 N.Y.C. arena
4 With 6-Across, semester-ending events for college students
6 See 4-Across
7 Bamboozled
8 The "p" in m.p.h.

DOWN

1 Confusion of one thing for another
2 Alan Rickman's role in the "Harry Potter" films
3 League of Legends player, e.g.
4 Gave dinner
5 Another name for acid

82

ACROSS

1 Try
8 Voice of Carl in Pixar's "Up"
9 "Heavens to Betsy!"
10 Fo' _____ (definitely, in slang)
11 Show with the coffeeshop Central Perk
15 It's abbreviated "RT" on social media
16 Epic poem by Homer

DOWN

1 _____ and haw
2 Suffix with Gator or Power
3 Goal for a high school athlete
4 Avoids using
5 "It's _____ guess at this point"
6 Precious stone
7 Resource in the game Settlers of Catan
11 To and _____
12 Side in checkers
13 Letter after cee
14 Pig's home

ACROSS

1 "To Kill a Mockingbird" author
4 With 7-Across, traditional holder of a president's assets
6 Monday, to the French
7 See 4-Across
8 Gratuitous feature of many HBO shows

DOWN

1 Operating system with a penguin logo
2 Discontinues
3 Rework, as an article
4 Sandwiches that usually contain mayo
5 Entice

84

ACROSS

1 Acronym for a controversial North Dakota oil carrier
5 Nine-headed monster of myth
6 Divvy up
7 "I love," in French
8 Folder for unread emails

DOWN

1 Bob who won the 2016 Nobel Prize for Literature
2 Wing it on stage
3 Teaser ad
4 Hospital glove material
5 Pilgrim to Mecca

	1	2	3	4
5				
6				
7				
8				

ACROSS

1 Bad ____ (negative vibes)
5 Brightest star in the constellation Cygnus
6 Beethoven's "Für ____"
7 ____ + water = bread
8 Lots and lots

DOWN

1 Kind of party shot that needs to set in the fridge
2 The "U" of the E.U.
3 Nativity scene baby
4 Company experimenting with self-driving cars
5 Skillful

ACROSS

1 Community that Ellen DeGeneres and Janet Mock are a part of
5 Bay ____ (Oakland's locale)
6 Italian restaurant basketful
7 Finished
8 Prop for Harry Potter

DOWN

1 Insect stage
2 Party for Jill Stein
3 Many a hipster has one
4 Little bit
6 Arrow shooter

1	2	3		
4			5	6
7				
8				
		9		

ACROSS
1 Pac-12 powerhouse
4 Steep drop-off on a mountain
7 Corporate department that reviews contracts
8 No longer sleeping
9 "Oedipus ___"

DOWN
1 Pac-12 powerhouse
2 Seattle ___ (Triple Crown winner)
3 Cuban smoke
5 Fraudulent
6 Show off one's muscles

ACROSS

1 Something that's non-PC?
4 Free-for-all fight
7 Second half of a musical
8 Cause of panic to beachgoers
9 Once called, in wedding notices

DOWN

1 Wharton School grads
2 St. Louis monument
3 Settlers of ___ (board game)
5 Something a police informant might wear
6 Filler word akin to "er" or "um"

ACROSS

1 Places to hibernate
6 Share : Facebook :: ____ : Twitter
8 Become frozen, as a plane's wings
9 Christmas Eve cuisine for Jews, it's said
10 "Purple Haze" guitarist
11 Leader of a 2016 recount effort
12 Miner's target

DOWN

1 Creepy old guys, slangily
2 Chipped away at
3 "Hmm . . ."
4 Daydream
5 Greets at the door
6 Among the 1%, so to speak
7 "Jurassic Park" dino

90

1	**2**	**3**	**4**	
5				**6**
7				
8				
	9			

ACROSS

1 Invoice for payment . . . or something to pay with
5 Cause of tears in the kitchen
7 Like dough that needs more kneading
8 Land on one side of Mt. Everest
9 How-____ (instruction books)

DOWN

1 Keep from moving . . . or move quickly
2 Alaskan native
3 Bend over backwards under a bar
4 Bounds along
6 "All the news that's fit to print" paper: Abbr.

ACROSS

1 Tit for ___
4 One-half of a 21st-century political duo
6 One-half of a 21st-century political duo
7 Rather cold, weatherwise
8 Results of using Tinder, hopefully

DOWN

1 Bone that's parallel to the fibula
2 Modify
3 Home to Arizona State University
4 007
5 No votes

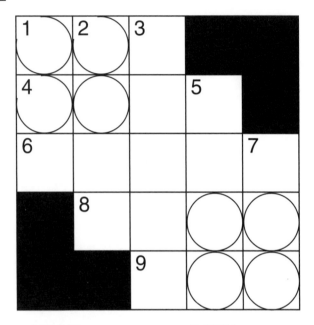

ACROSS

1 Business-focused daily, briefly
4 Heavy load
6 "___ bet?"
8 Subatomic particle whose name is derived from a Greek letter
9 Pained reactions

DOWN

1 "Holy cow!"
2 Ginger cookie
3 Sixth Spanish month
5 Balls of it are found in this puzzle
7 Part of Q&A: Abbr.

ACROSS

1 Fancy party
5 Jesse who won four golds at the Berlin Olympics
7 Hanukkah treat
8 Ali vs. Frazier, e.g.
9 Chuck

DOWN

1 Game with chips and aces
2 Look forward to
3 Release one's grip
4 Old Egyptian crosses
6 Tennis match parts

1	2	3	4	5
6				
7				
8				
9				

ACROSS

1 "Go on, git!"
6 Country adjacent to the Dominican Republic
7 Finger you point with
8 "___ One: A Star Wars Story"
9 Hangs onto

DOWN

1 Avoid, as responsibility
2 Craft with a paddle
3 Crested part of a mountain
4 Consumed with gusto
5 Shuffles or jumbles

ACROSS

1 Ocean liner?
5 Buzzing musical toy
6 Russian leader with a black belt in judo
7 White Monopoly bills
8 Walk back and forth

DOWN

1 Steam room
2 Ancient Mexican pyramid builder
3 What earplugs block out
4 "___ we now our gay apparel"
5 Genre for Psy's "Gangnam Style," informally

ACROSS

1 Londoner or Liverpudlian, e.g.
5 Somewhat: Prefix
6 Crossword, for one
7 Formed into tight curls, as hair
8 Roofed patios (hint: from the Hawaiian)
9 Love to pieces
10 Animal said to cause warts

DOWN

1 Bird circling above a carcass
2 Award for the worst movie of the year
3 Micronesia is made up of them
4 Deadlocked
5 Grain that's popular among the health-conscious
6 Madrid art museum
7 Having a slope of zero

				■
1	2	3	4	
5				6
7				
8				
■	9			

ACROSS

1 Something that's checked twice, in a Christmas song
5 Residue on 8-Across's suit after fitting through the chimney
7 Air Force One, e.g.
8 Traveler on Christmas Eve
9 Event held at midnight on Christmas Eve

DOWN

1 Runners and swimmers do them
2 Malcolm X's faith
3 ___ Alexander, pioneering female journalist
4 Campers' shelters
6 Seven ___

98

ACROSS

1 With 5-Down, novel that begins "Call me Ishmael"
5 Birds in "Twelve Days of Christmas"
6 Counting everything
7 ___-Alt-Del
8 Alt and Delete, e.g.

DOWN

1 Three-card scam
2 Female reproductive gland
3 "Jingle ___"
4 Fashion monogram
5 See 1-Across

1	2	3	4	5
6				
7				
8				
9				

ACROSS

1 Book obviated by Google Earth
6 One who you get tongue-tied around, maybe
7 Hulking African mammal
8 More slippery, as a ski run
9 Tube-shaped pasta

DOWN

1 Have ____ on one's shoulder
2 In a ____ (very quickly)
3 Hogwarts professor who's actually a werewolf
4 Colorado ski resort
5 Place to look for seashells

100

	1	2	3	4
5				
6				
7				
8				■

ACROSS
1 Hard Rock ___
5 Pilot portrayed by Tom Hanks
6 Speak into a drive-thru mic, say
7 Girl who cries "Uncle!"
8 Part of N.Y.C.

DOWN
1 Unusual object
2 Tree in the birch family
3 Tiny patch of color
4 Jane ___, Brontë heroine
5 PlayStation 4 maker

1	2	3	4	5
6				
7				
8				
9				

ACROSS

1 Many an auto plant worker, nowadays
6 Like hares, but not hairs
7 "Hard" apple drink
8 2, 4, 6, 8, etc.
9 Like the center of a black hole

DOWN

1 Competed in a 5K
2 Pizza topping
3 Name on a 2008 bumper sticker
4 Pizzerias use them
5 Verbally to the point

ACROSS

1 1980s pop duo with George Michael
5 Dance party with glowsticks, maybe
6 Triangular road sign
8 It has rings and shoots
9 Something on the agenda

DOWN

1 Dryly humorous
2 Country founded after a slave revolt
3 Turn away, as one's gaze
4 Free-for-all
7 One in a blue state majority, for short

ACROSS

1 Hindu deity
5 "Great blue" bird
6 Expel from a country
7 They can determine who makes the team
8 Wide-ranging adventure
9 President ___ (Senate position)
10 "Green Eggs and Ham" author

DOWN

1 Shares, as another's Facebook status
2 Stimulates
3 Post-___ analysis
4 Unable to sit still
5 "Oh my god, look who it is!"
6 Rapper who created the Beats headphones
7 Blouses and T-shirts, e.g.

104

ACROSS

1 With 7-Across and 5-Down, time to make resolutions

4 Scent of a tree-shaped air freshener

5 River's mouth

6 ___ Iverson, N.B.A. Hall-of-Famer

7 See 1-Across

DOWN

1 Nabisco's ___ wafers

2 Type in

3 Gradually makes less dependent

4 One-named Brazilian soccer legend

5 See 1-Across

ACROSS

1 Sagacious
5 Array on a computer dock
7 Colin who won an Oscar for "The King's Speech"
8 First paragraph of an essay, informally
9 "I Heard It Through the Grapevine" singer

DOWN

1 Amenity in many an airport
2 Sugar coat?
3 "I mean . . . you're basically right"
4 Contest submission
6 Loafer or sneaker

106

ACROSS
1 Each of the O's in XOXO
4 Divided Asian land
6 IDs on library books
7 Biting, smug tone
8 Certain trig ratios

DOWN
1 _____ Mubarak, onetime Egyptian ruler
2 Word before legend and dictionary
3 Literature category
4 Each of the X's on XOXO
5 Questions

ACROSS
1 Soft rock?
5 "Wouldn't that be nice!"
7 Smith who wrote the 2016 bestseller "Swing Time"
8 Height × width calculations
9 Crime bosses

DOWN
1 Minnelli with an Emmy and Grammy
2 Emmy or Grammy
3 YouTube posting
4 Cuisine category on Seamless
6 Toy truck maker

ACROSS

1 Sign of auto body aging
5 With 1-Down, defining book of the Beat generation
7 Add fancy accessories to
8 Ate elegantly
9 What's in the middle of "middle"

DOWN

1 See 5-Across
2 Reversed
3 Something skipped across a pond
4 Rough approximation of pi
6 Odds and ____

ACROSS

1 Weirdly, its state bird is the California gull
5 Blandly average, in modern lingo
7 Privileged few
8 Complete startovers
9 Gmail outbox folder

DOWN

1 Lyft competitor
2 "The Canterbury ___"
3 Line that breaks the fourth wall
4 Flirt with
6 "___ la vie!"

110

ACROSS

1 T.S.A. agents request them
4 Steps on a banana peel, say
6 Teen loitering around a shopping center
8 Make louder
9 By the sea
10 ___-backwards
11 Before, in poetry
12 Used to be
13 "Aaron Burr, ___" ("Hamilton" song with a rhyming title)

DOWN

1 "None for me, thanks"
2 Popular pickles
3 Alternatives to 7UPs
4 Stuffed Indian appetizer
5 Wild vacation?
6 Parrot with a large beak
7 First president who wasn't elected

1	**2**	**3**	**4**	
5				
6				**7**
	8			
	9			

ACROSS

1 Like Tommy in the Who's rock opera "Tommy"
5 Bush's Axis of ___
6 Penny pincher
8 Board game with six suspects
9 Maryland player, for short

DOWN

1 One on the left side of 3-Down: Abbr.
2 Kick out, as a tenant
3 Congressional divide
4 ___-de-lis
7 One on the right side of 3-Down: Abbr.

112

	1	2	3	4
5				
6				
7				
8				

ACROSS

1 Pokémon Go and the Mannequin Challenge, in 2016
5 Paris transit system
6 Totally committed
7 Like "turnt" and "bae"
8 To-do list item

DOWN

1 Guy
2 Book of maps
3 Compete in beer pong or flip cup, say
4 Any one of the Top 40
5 Crow's-nest spot

1	2	3	4	■
5				6
7				
8				
■	9			

ACROSS

1 Summer getaway for kids
5 Mr. T series, with "The"
7 Speaking platforms
8 Try to hit a golf ball
9 Launcher of the Curiosity rover

DOWN

1 Uppercase letters, informally
2 Nickname for the capital of Georgia
3 Industry for the New York Times
4 Aches and ____
6 Acronym in many a Donald Trump tweet

114

ACROSS

1 Waiter's handout
5 With 6-Across, column left of the decimal
6 See 5-Across
7 Bulletin board fastener
8 The "A" of B.A.

DOWN

1 Grinding tooth
2 Make into law
3 Sites of some massages
4 "___ with caution"
6 Back-to-school night grp.

	1	2	3	4
	5			
6				
7				
8				

ACROSS

1 It's a portmanteau, but not for "small dog"
5 ___ Alto, Calif.
6 One-named singer with the 2013 #1 hit "Royals"
7 First astrological sign
8 It's a portmanteau, but not for "ski resort"

DOWN

1 It's a portmanteau, but not for "salt pork"
2 Plumber in Nintendo games
3 Like Beyoncé, vis-à-vis Solange Knowles
4 Proceed, in Biblical English
6 The "L" of U.N.L.V.

116

1	2	3	4	5
6				
7				
8				
9				

ACROSS

1 Related to Francis and the Vatican
6 Food-poisoning bacteria
7 Puzzlemaker with a famous cube
8 Treasure ___ (motherlode)
9 Chris who hosts on MSNBC

DOWN

1 City on Australia's western coast
2 Rival of Lexus
3 Fried shrimp sandwich
4 Having a pulse
5 Positive reactions to a Facebook post

1	2	3	4	5
6				
7				
8				
9				

ACROSS

1 Site with a Symptom Checker feature
6 Dropping a pop fly, for example
7 Silly and pointless
8 Basmati and jasmine
9 "Give me the ___!" (slangy request for info)

DOWN

1 Bizarre
2 Bert's pal on "Sesame Street"
3 Wear after a knee injury
4 French painter of "Water Lilies"
5 Prom purchase, for some

118

	1	2	3	4
5				
6				
7				
8				

ACROSS

1 Food that often comes in small cubes
5 ‾_(ツ)_/‾
6 Put ____ on it (propose, slangily)
7 Brightly-lit signs
8 Say no to

DOWN

1 Goals in a hat trick
2 Constellation with a "belt"
3 Like articles in The Onion
4 Fleece-lined boots
5 Hourglass filler

1	2	3	4	■
5				6
7				
8				
■	9			

ACROSS
1 The 13 and 17, in PG-13 and NC-17
5 Annoys greatly
7 Counting everything
8 Country estate
9 Website that offers homemade crafts

DOWN
1 Tel ___, Israel
2 One granting three wishes
3 Glorify
4 Puts on eBay, maybe
6 Defeat, as a dragon

ACROSS
1 "A rabbi, a priest and a duck walk into ___ . . ."
5 National park in Alaska with a GMC truck namesake
7 National park in Utah named for a geological formation
8 Native American people with a California desert named for them
9 Stadium toppers
10 Period in history

DOWN
1 Anderson Cooper or Jake Tapper
2 ___ mama (rhyming rum drink)
3 Pain reliever brand
4 Goes up
5 River blocker
6 Wash away, as soil

ACROSS

1 Like steak tartare and sashimi
4 Punk, rock or folk
6 Segment of a comic strip
7 Popular office communication software
8 Honoree on Jan. 16, 2017

DOWN

1 King's domain
2 Record of the year's events
3 Demolish
4 Car navigation aid, for short
5 Antlered animal

ACROSS

1 What "lento" means on a music score
5 Shanghai's home
6 Metropolitan
7 Shocking, like a tabloid headline
8 Way up a ski slope

DOWN

1 Synonym for bush that contains the letters B, U, S, and H
2 Zodiac sign after Virgo
3 Currently being broadcast
4 Something waved by a T.S.A. agent
5 ____ of personality

123

	1	2	3	
4				5
6				
7				
8				

ACROSS

1 Energy
4 Gin's partner in a classic drink
6 Jerry Jones for the Dallas Cowboys, e.g.
7 Tennis tie
8 Like prunes and raisins

DOWN

1 Electricity
2 Feeling of weariness towards life
3 Part of a jigsaw puzzle
4 Chuck who hosts "Meet the Press"
5 Street ___ (respect)

124

ACROSS

1 "Don't worry about me!"
5 Piglike South American mammal
7 Bush's vice president
9 Sad-looking, as a facial expression
11 "C'mon, I'm trying to leave"
12 Scheduled to arrive
13 Zap with a stun gun

DOWN

1 Symptom of a mosquito bite
2 Taj ___
3 Began playing in theaters
4 Pharaoh whose artifacts have toured the world
6 Body of water parted by Moses
8 Practitioners of Hatha, Ashtanga or Bikram
10 "___ fishing" (quaint store sign)

ACROSS

1 In the 70's, temperaturewise
5 Fencing blade
6 Protest in Washington D.C., say
7 Reebok competitor
8 App for looking up nearby restaurants

DOWN

1 Zig and zag while driving
2 It comes between 6-Across and 6-Down
3 Summary of a sports game
4 "It was so-so"
6 Could possibly

126

ACROSS

1 Nervous swallow
5 "This can't be good!"
6 Flannel shirt pattern
7 Hurtful word
8 Bit of land surrounded by ocean

DOWN

1 Birds at the beach
2 Big name in personal moving vans
3 Longest river entirely in France
4 Grad school degree
6 Greek letter after chi

ACROSS

1 Smooch
5 Spiral seashell
6 Medium for Rush Limbaugh
7 "___ it at home" (homework excuse)
8 Competitor of an Uber car

DOWN

1 Cuddly-looking marsupial
2 Section at the back of a textbook
3 Genre for TV's "Stranger Things"
4 Three-pointer or layup
5 Lit ___ (English course, colloquially)

128

		1	2	3
4	5			
6				
7				
8				

ACROSS

1 Minuscule
4 Little
6 "___ and conditions may apply"
7 Get up
8 Prefix with thermal

DOWN

1 Nintendo villain in purple suspenders
2 Trees that line the National Mall
3 "If all ___ fails . . ."
4 Doe's mate
5 Trifling

1	2	3	4	
5				
6				7
	8			
	9			

ACROSS
1 What a spoiler spoils
5 In addition
6 Iconic jogger up the Philadelphia Museum of Art stairs
8 "Divine Secrets of the ___ Sisterhood"
9 Bit of rain

DOWN
1 Good golf score
2 Architect Frank ___ Wright
3 Academy Award
4 City with the largest population (37+ million)
7 Sound from a tiny dog

ACROSS

1 Google result
4 Blow, as a volcano
7 Home for "The Colbert Report," but not "The Late Show With Stephen Colbert"
8 The bee's ___ (very cool)
9 Snitch

DOWN

1 Mild expletive
2 Its capital is Tehran
3 Yam or sweet potato
5 "Not guilty," e.g.
6 The "T" of LSAT

ACROSS

1 Like one texting :'-(
4 With 13-Across, annual lunar celebration
8 Cola container
9 Not post-
10 Groove in a muddy road
11 ____ Fuqua, director of "Training Day"
13 See 4-Across
14 British reference work, for short

DOWN

1 Other half of a cassette
2 Santa ____ winds
3 Condemned openly
4 Airer of Congressional hearings
5 Singer Lena with four Grammys and a Tony
6 Place to sweat it out
7 Type in
12 "____ Como Va"

132

ACROSS

1 Hit with an open palm
5 Basis for a lawsuit
6 Trivia fodder
7 Annoys
8 "50 Shades of ___"

DOWN

1 Drummer who played with McCartney and Harrison
2 English philosopher John
3 Pretentiously highbrow
4 Six are awarded for a touchdown: Abbr.
6 Fruit mentioned in Genesis

ACROSS

1 "Forgot About ___" (rap classic)
4 Like 60% of humankind
6 Brilliant, as colors
7 Removes the wrinkles from
8 Gain a lap?

DOWN

1 Chunk out of the fairway, in golf
2 Desert rarity
3 Comes to a close
4 Car rental option
5 iPhone assistant

134

ACROSS

1 Smile ear to ear
5 Military force
6 Constant complainer
8 Jacob's twin, in the Bible
9 Bit of damage to a car bumper

DOWN

1 Baseball base
2 Made a mistake
3 Cause to chuckle
4 "Nice going, dude!"
7 "To ___ it mildly . . ."

ACROSS

1 Channel that started the reality boom with "Real World"
4 Drug recovery program
6 Avoid
7 Icy streaker in space
8 "All Things Considered" airer

DOWN

1 Cantaloupe or honeydew
2 Loud, dull sound
3 "Star Wars" villain
4 ___ center (community facility)
5 Poker action

136

ACROSS
1 Being number one?
5 Once more than once
6 Once more
7 Pebble-like candy from Wonka
8 Target of a frantic search when leaving the house

DOWN
1 "How sweet!," in an old-fashioned way
2 Book with personal entries
3 Low-pH substances
4 Restroom door word
5 Armored vehicle with a gun mount

	1	2	3	4
5				
6				
7				
8				■

ACROSS

1 Politico Sessions
5 One throwing jabs and hooks
6 Loosen, as shoelaces
7 L, on a T-shirt tag
8 Khizr ___, noted speaker at the 2016 Democratic Convention

DOWN

1 Biblical figure swallowed by a whale
2 When doubled, old newsboy's cry
3 Pretend
4 Costing nothing
5 Major portion

1	**2**	**3**	■	**4**	**5**	**6**
7			**8**			
9						
■	**10**					■
11						**12**
13						
14			■	**15**		

ACROSS

1 Egyptian snake
4 Move like a bunny
7 Those going from fat to fit, say
9 Bill who co-wrote "Killing Lincoln" and "Killing Kennedy"
10 Woolly sight in the Andes
11 Jewelry that goes on the foot
13 Lin-Manuel who created "Hamilton"
14 ___ and outs
15 Grp. symbolized by an elephant

DOWN

1 "Much ___ About Nothing"
2 Prime beef cut
3 Kitchen tools used for preparing potatoes
4 Steering, as a ship
5 Home to Disney World
6 "Gangnam Style" rapper
8 Bejeweled headgear
11 "OMG, spare me the details!"
12 Opening

ACROSS

1 That woman
4 Tom ___, quarterback in Super Bowl LI
6 Widespread fad
7 Add more lanes to, as a highway
8 Cunning

DOWN

1 Useful
2 Falco of "The Sopranos"
3 Matt ___, quarterback in Super Bowl LI
4 High-end German cars
5 Amtrak track

140

1	2	3	4	5
6				
7				
8				
9				

ACROSS

1 Michigan city with a water crisis
6 Shakespearean character mentioned in Taylor Swift's "Love Story"
7 One of the Coen brothers
8 Took illegally
9 Person who's always trying to bring you down

DOWN

1 "Certified ___" (Rotten Tomatoes distinction)
2 Bunch of, slangily
3 Comment made while fanning oneself
4 Writer Zora ___ Hurston
5 Ink for a laser printer

	1	2	3	4
5				
6				
7				
8				

ACROSS
1 Offerings in the Google Play store
5 Perfect
6 2:1 or 4:3
7 Growing older
8 Protections against mosquitoes

DOWN
1 Memorable saying
2 Small, to the French
3 Aches and ____
4 Long, boring task
5 Country that borders three -stans

142

ACROSS
1 Comes to a close
5 U.S. politician who won the 2007 Nobel Peace Prize
6 Like spanakopita and feta cheese
8 "G'day ____!"
9 Beijing air problem

DOWN
1 "Which came first?" item
2 Usual practices
3 Frequent occurrence during REM sleep
4 Take care of
7 Beer holder for a big party

ACROSS

1 College transcript nos.
5 Francis, for one
6 Always in a bad mood
8 What the 5-Across is bishop of
9 Disappearing photo on a popular app

DOWN

1 Car's navigational tool, for short
2 Transfers from pitcher to glass
3 Chef's wear
4 Alabama march city
7 "Sure thing"

ACROSS

1 Football players wear them
5 Drink like a dog
6 Another name for a stimulant drug
7 Rapper with the 2003 #1 hit "Shake Ya Tailfeather"
8 Greek god of war

DOWN

1 Loser to scissors, in a classic game
2 Fruit that inspired Newton, supposedly
3 Face-offs in the Wild West
4 Quick on one's feet
5 Roman goddess of the moon

ACROSS

1 Breadcrumb carrier
4 Sony rival
7 Product from Dove or Dial
9 Kristen who recently hosted "S.N.L."
10 Result of a coin flip
11 British meat pies
13 Piled up, like dirty clothes
14 Cough medicine amt.
15 Home for a hog

DOWN

1 Stomach muscles
2 Fast-food company with an annual hot dog eating competition
3 Syrup source
4 They travel with the band
5 Infant's place when driving
6 Fitting
8 Large strip
11 Center of a peach
12 One who's always bugging people?

146

ACROSS

1 Guns, as an engine
5 The South, affectionately
6 Offering at New York's Lincoln Center
7 Any episode of "Seinfeld," now
8 Insects in "A Bug's Life"

DOWN

1 Turn red, as strawberries
2 Put forth, as effort
3 Attachment on a sketchy email
4 White House press secretary Spicer
5 ___ the Explorer

ACROSS

1 ___ Club (Costco competitor)
5 Leather bottoms
7 Alphabet quintet
8 Lord's estate
9 Fake out in the rink

DOWN

1 Pyramid scheme or three-card monte
2 "Full speed ___!"
3 Only U.S. state with a monosyllabic name
4 Scare
6 "No problem!"

148

ACROSS

1 "Every kiss begins with . . ." jeweler
4 Gooey campfire treat
6 Valentine's Day symbol
7 Capital of Norway
8 Remove from the freezer

DOWN

1 Australian "bear"
2 Cupid's dart
3 "You ain't seen nothin' ___"
4 Let loose, as a 2-Down
5 Fit nicely (with)

1	2	3	4	5
6				
7				
8				
9				

ACROSS

1 Musical symbols meaning "silence"
6 Lexus rival
7 Someone seen on a runway
8 Something seen on a runway
9 Shoots off, as an email

DOWN

1 Freeway entrances
2 French for "school"
3 African country that's majority Muslim
4 Be popular, as a Twitter hashtag
5 "Everything must go!" events

	1	2	3	4
5				
6				
7				
8				

ACROSS

1 Foolish
5 Prefix with brewery or economics
6 No longer working for a U.S. intelligence grp.
7 Buenos ___, capital of Argentina
8 Opposite of most

DOWN

1 Big name in paper cups
2 Capital of Ghana
3 French ___ (side order)
4 French ___ (breakfast order)
5 Breakfast, lunch or dinner

ANSWERS

1

B	U	S	■	
A	B	A	C	K
R	E	T	R	O
T	R	A	I	N
■		N	B	A

2

I	N	C	■	
H	O	U	R	S
O	R	B	I	T
P	I	E	C	E
■		D	E	W

3

■	D	A	F	T
J	E	L	L	O
A	L	L	I	N
I	V	O	R	Y
N	E	W	T	■

4

	C	A	F	E
	A	C	I	D
R	I	T	Z	Y
D	R	O	Z	
S	O	N	Y	

5

		P	A	D		
	S	O	L	E	S	
B	O	L	I	V	I	A
U	N	I	T	I	N	G
G	O	T	T	A	G	O
	F	I	L	T	H	
	C	E	E			

6

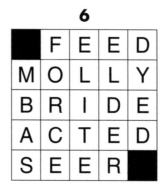

	F	E	E	D
M	O	L	L	Y
B	R	I	D	E
A	C	T	E	D
S	E	E	R	

7

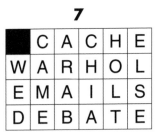

	C	A	C	H	E
W	A	R	H	O	L
E	M	A	I	L	S
D	E	B	A	T	E

8

R	B	I	S	
S	U	G	A	R
V	I	L	L	A
P	L	O	T	Z
	D	O	S	E

9

A	L	I	S	T
D	A	N	T	E
O	U	T	E	D
B	R	E	A	D
E	A	R	L	Y

10

	S	A	L	T
M	I	M	E	O
E	X	P	A	T
S	T	E	V	E
H	Y	D	E	

11

I	P	A		
C	O	L	I	N
K	N	I	F	E
Y	E	A	S	T
		S	O	S

12

			J	E	F	F
		M	O	V	E	R
	M	A	H	A	L	O
C	O	R	N	D	O	G
A	R	I	S	E	N	
M	A	N	O	R		
P	L	A	N			

13

	D	I	S	
V	E	N	M	O
I	N	T	O	W
N	I	E	C	E
	M	L	K	

14

	L	E	F	T
W	A	X	E	R
R	U	P	E	E
A	R	O	L	E
P	A	S	S	

15

S	A	C	K	
P	L	A	N	E
A	P	R	E	S
W	H	E	L	P
N	A	S	T	Y

16

	P	U	S	H
P	A	R	T	Y
A	L	B	U	M
L	E	A	N	N
S	O	N	G	

17

M	A	N		
O	B	A	M	A
J	C	R	E	W
O	S	C	A	R
		S	L	Y

18

S	N	A	K	E
N	O	T	A	X
A	T	T	I	C
P	I	A	N	O
S	T	R	E	P

19

		P	A	C	T
		H	O	C	H	I
	T	O	U	C	A	N
P	H	O	T	O	I	D
A	R	T	I	S	T	E
R	E	E	N	T	E	R
T	E	R	E	S	A	

20

	A	S	H	
F	L	E	A	S
A	L	E	V	E
L	A	Y	E	R
L	H	A	S	A

21

W	A	L	D	O
O	R	C	A	S
M	E	D	I	A
E	N	T	R	Y
N	A	V	Y	

22

	S	E	A	S
K	A	B	U	L
E	M	O	J	I
G	O	O	U	T
S	A	K	S	

23

A	M	T		
R	E	A	C	H
C	O	C	O	A
S	W	I	M	S
		T	B	H

24

P	E		A	S
L	A	S	I	K
A	T	A	R	I
C	E	D	E	D
E	N		D	S

25

S	U	V		
P	H	I	S	H
A	O	R	T	A
S	H	A	U	N
		L	B	S

26

L	I	B	E	L	
I	T	U	N	E	S
S	A	R	A	N	A	C
A	L	I	B	A	B	A
	Y	E	L	P	E	R
		D	E	E	R	E

27

	C	A	S	E
B	O	L	T	S
O	N	T	O	P
O	V	A	R	Y
N	O	R	M	

28

A	R	D	O	R
W	E	A	R	Y
E	L	I	T	E
D	A	L	I	S
■	X	Y	Z	■

29

■	G	O	L	F
P	U	R	E	E
L	A	B	E	L
E	V	I	C	T
B	A	T	H	■

30

A	L	A	S	■
T	I	L	E	■
A	F	T	E	R
D	E	A	T	H
■	■	R	O	O

31

R	U	N	G	
A	M	I	E	
N	A	F	T	A
	S	T	I	R
	S	Y	N	C

32

	M	I	T	
Z	E	B	R	A
I	D	I	O	M
G	I	Z	M	O
	C	A	P	

33

	S	L	A	C	K
	L	E	B	R	O	N
P	O	R	S	C	H	E
A	M	P		H	E	E
D	E	E	P	E	N	D
M	I	N	O	R	S	
E	N	T	R	Y		

34

C	H	R	I	S
R	O	U	T	E
A	W	M	A	N
I	T	O	L	D
G	O	R	Y	

35

	C	H	E	M
	H	U	L	U
L	I	M	O	S
I	N	I	N	K
P	A	D		

36

L	A	T	C	H
A	L	O	H	A
P	I	T	A	S
A	V	E	R	T
Z	E	S	T	Y

37

	P	E	A	K
B	I	G	L	Y
A	N	G	E	L
S	T	O	R	E
K	A	N	T	

38

R	A	M	P	
A	D	O	U	T
C	A	R	T	A
E	M	A	I	L
	S	Y	N	C

39

D	R	O	Z	
V	O	W	E	L
D	O	L	B	Y
S	T	E	R	N
	S	T	A	X

40

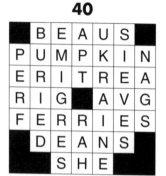

```
  B E A U S
P U M P K I N
E R I T R E A
R I G   A V G
F E R R I E S
  D E A N S
    S H E
```

41

```
  W I S H
W I L L Y
I S L A M
M E G Y N
P R O S
```

42

```
    H O P
S C A R E
H O U S E
O R N O T
T N T
```

43

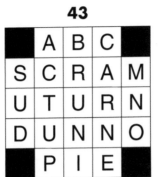

	A	B	C	
S	C	R	A	M
U	T	U	R	N
D	U	N	N	O
	P	I	E	

44

	W	H	E	W
	H	U	M	A
M	O	M	M	Y
P	L	O	Y	
H	E	R	S	

45

C	O	L	D	
U	B	E	R	S
B	A	D	A	T
S	M	O	K	E
	A	N	E	W

46

		J	F	K
S	H	A	L	E
C	O	M	E	Y
O	P	E	D	S
T	I	S		

47

		V	I	P	
C	L	I	N	I	C	S
R	O	O	F	T	O	P
A	I	L		S	L	O
C	R	E	A	T	O	R
K	E	N	B	O	N	E
		T	A	P		

48

I	O	W	A	
T	B	A	L	L
C	I	L	I	A
H	E	L	E	N
	S	E	N	D

49

M	O	C	H	I
A	C	H	E	D
G	E	O	D	E
M	A	N	G	A
A	N	G	E	L

50

■	V	O	T	E
N	I	G	H	T
E	L	L	I	S
E	L	E	G	Y
D	A	S	H	■

51

■	H	A	R	P
■	O	B	O	E
D	R	U	M	S
O	N	S	E	T
E	S	E	■	■

52

A	I	D		
C	O	U	P	S
T	W	E	E	T
S	A	L	S	A
		S	O	Y

53

	N	E	W	
C	A	R	O	B
B	A	R	R	Y
S	C	O	R	E
	P	R	Y	

54

	P	J	S		
	M	I	A	T	A
B	A	N	K	I	N	G
R	I	H	A	N	N	A
B	E	E	R	G	U	T
	R	A	T	E	S	
	D	A	R		

55

	T	A	L	E
S	O	L	I	D
O	K	I	N	G
O	Y	V	E	Y
T	O	E	S	

56

C	H	E	W	
H	A	B	I	T
O	Z	O	N	E
P	E	N	C	E
	L	Y	E	S

57

	M	V	P	S
D	A	I	L	Y
A	P	R	O	N
F	L	U	T	E
T	E	S	S	

58

	T	A	S	
S	O	U	T	H
I	N	D	I	A
T	A	I	L	S
S	L	O	T	H

59

	A	L	P	S
	S	H	O	O
C	O	A	L	S
U	R	S	A	
B	E	A	R	

60

S	H	A	F	T
C	A	D	R	E
A	D	E	U	X
R	E	L	I	T
F	R	E	T	S

61

S	A	T		R	C	T
P	R	I	M	E	R	O
O	M	N	I	B	U	S
T	E	A	S	E	S	
I	N	F	E	C	T	S
F	I	E	R	C	E	R
Y	A	Y		A	D	S

62

	A	L	I	S
	C	O	C	O
D	U	G	I	N
I	R	A	N	
Y	A	N	G	

63

F	O	B	S	
A	C	R	I	D
K	E	A	N	U
E	A	V	E	D
	N	E	W	S

64

D	A	K	A	R
W	R	I	T	E
A	I	D	E	S
R	A	D	I	I
F	L	Y	N	N

65

G	E	C	K	O
E	T	H	E	R
S	H	O	N	E
T	O	K	Y	O
■	S	E	A	S

66

■	U	C	S	F
■	N	A	T	O
T	H	R	E	E
D	I	V	E	■
S	P	E	D	■

67

	A	B	B	A
	P	R	O	S
T	H	I	G	H
W	I	N	G	
O	D	E	S	

68

		S	L	E	D	S
	R	O	T	T	E	N
B	U	R	R	I	T	O
A	M	C		C	O	O
S	P	E	A	K	U	P
T	U	R	N	E	R	
A	S	Y	E	T		

69

C	H	A	D	S
R	O	S	I	N
I	M	A	G	E
M	E	D	I	A
P	R	A	N	K

70

M	E	D	S	■
A	L	E	C	■
R	I	V	E	R
■	Z	I	N	E
■	A	L	E	X

71

■	G	A	G	A
S	E	O	U	L
A	N	K	L	E
C	R	A	P	S
K	E	Y	S	■

72

B	U	F	F	■
A	V	I	A	N
R	U	B	I	O
E	L	E	N	A
D	A	R	T	H

73

	B	A	I	T
S	E	N	S	E
E	A	G	L	E
M	U	L	A	N
I	T	E	M	S

74

	S	T	E	P
	N	U	N	S
P	A	N	D	A
O	R	E	O	
T	E	R	N	

75

	C	H	A	P	
	H	A	R	A	S	S
D	E	N	T	Y	N	E
R	E	D		R	A	N
U	S	B	P	O	R	T
B	E	A	G	L	E	
	G	A	L	S	

76

S	P	I	T	■
O	I	L	Y	
L	O	O	P	Y
■	U	V	E	A
	S	E	A	M

77

S	T	I	R	S
M	I	T	E	S
I	M	E	A	N
T	E	M	P	S
E	S	S	■	

78

L	O	L	■	■
E	X	U	R	B
E	E	R	I	E
K	N	I	F	E
■		D	E	R

79

	G	U	S	H
F	E	N	C	E
U	N	I	O	N
T	I	T	U	S
Z	E	S	T	

80

		J	E	D
T	H	E	R	E
O	A	S	I	S
T	R	U	C	K
O	K	S		

81

	M	S	G	
F	I	N	A	L
E	X	A	M	S
D	U	P	E	D
	P	E	R	

82

H	A	V	E	A	G	O
E	D	A	S	N	E	R
M	E	R	C	Y	M	E
■		S	H	O		■
F	R	I	E	N	D	S
R	E	T	W	E	E	T
O	D	Y	S	S	E	Y

83

■		L	E	E
B	L	I	N	D
L	U	N	D	I
T	R	U	S	T
S	E	X	■	

84

■	D	A	P	L
H	Y	D	R	A
A	L	L	O	T
J	A	I	M	E
I	N	B	O	X

85

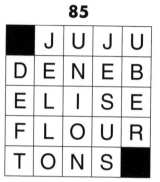

	J	U	J	U
D	E	N	E	B
E	L	I	S	E
F	L	O	U	R
T	O	N	S	

86

	L	G	B	T
A	R	E	A
B	R	E	A	D
O	V	E	R	
W	A	N	D	

87

U	S	C		
C	L	I	F	F
L	E	G	A	L
A	W	A	K	E
	R	E	X	

88

M	A	C		
B	R	A	W	L
A	C	T	I	I
S	H	A	R	K
		N	E	E

89

	L	A	I	R	S	
R	E	T	W	E	E	T
I	C	E	O	V	E	R
C	H	I	N	E	S	E
H	E	N	D	R	I	X
	S	T	E	I	N	
	O	R	E			

90

B	I	L	L	
O	N	I	O	N
L	U	M	P	Y
T	I	B	E	T
	T	O	S	

91

	T	A	T	
B	I	D	E	N
O	B	A	M	A
N	I	P	P	Y
D	A	T	E	S

92

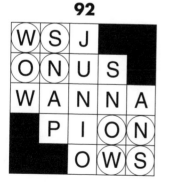

93

G	A	L	A	
O	W	E	N	S
L	A	T	K	E
F	I	G	H	T
	T	O	S	S

94

S	C	R	A	M
H	A	I	T	I
I	N	D	E	X
R	O	G	U	E
K	E	E	P	S

95

■	S	A	N	D
K	A	Z	O	O
P	U	T	I	N
O	N	E	S	■
P	A	C	E	■

96

■	■	B	R	I	T	
■	Q	U	A	S	I	
■	P	U	Z	Z	L	E
F	R	I	Z	Z	E	D
L	A	N	A	I	S	■
A	D	O	R	E	■	■
T	O	A	D	■	■	■

97

L	I	S	T	■
A	S	H	E	S
P	L	A	N	E
S	A	N	T	A
■	M	A	S	S

98

■	M	O	B	Y
D	O	V	E	S
I	N	A	L	L
C	T	R	L	■
K	E	Y	S	■

99

A	T	L	A	S
C	R	U	S	H
H	I	P	P	O
I	C	I	E	R
P	E	N	N	E

100

	C	A	F	E
S	U	L	L	Y
O	R	D	E	R
N	I	E	C	E
Y	O	R	K	

101

R	O	B	O	T
A	L	I	V	E
C	I	D	E	R
E	V	E	N	S
D	E	N	S	E

102

W	H	A	M	
R	A	V	E	
Y	I	E	L	D
	T	R	E	E
	I	T	E	M

103

			R	A	M	A
		H	E	R	O	N
	D	E	P	O	R	T
T	R	Y	O	U	T	S
O	D	Y	S	S	E	Y
P	R	O	T	E	M	
S	E	U	S	S		

104

	N	E	W
	P	I	N	E
D	E	L	T	A
A	L	L	E	N
Y	E	A	R	S

105

W	I	S	E	
I	C	O	N	S
F	I	R	T	H
I	N	T	R	O
	G	A	Y	E

106

	H	U	G	
K	O	R	E	A
I	S	B	N	S
S	N	A	R	K
S	I	N	E	S

107

L	A	V	A	
I	W	I	S	H
Z	A	D	I	E
A	R	E	A	S
	D	O	N	S

108

R	U	S	T	
O	N	T	H	E
A	D	O	R	N
D	I	N	E	D
	D	E	E	S

109

U	T	A	H	■
B	A	S	I	C
E	L	I	T	E
R	E	D	O	S
■	S	E	N	T

110

■	■	I	D	S	■	■
■	S	L	I	P	S	■
M	A	L	L	R	A	T
A	M	P	L	I	F	Y
C	O	A	S	T	A	L
A	S	S	■	E	R	E
W	A	S	■	S	I	R

111

D	E	A	F	■
E	V	I	L	■
M	I	S	E	R
■	C	L	U	E
■	T	E	R	P

112

	F	A	D	S
M	E	T	R	O
A	L	L	I	N
S	L	A	N	G
T	A	S	K	

113

C	A	M	P	
A	T	E	A	M
P	O	D	I	A
S	W	I	N	G
	N	A	S	A

114

	M	E	N	U
	O	N	E	S
P	L	A	C	E
T	A	C	K	
A	R	T	S	

115

	S	M	O	G
	P	A	L	O
L	O	R	D	E
A	R	I	E	S
S	K	O	R	T

116

P	A	P	A	L
E	C	O	L	I
R	U	B	I	K
T	R	O	V	E
H	A	Y	E	S

117

W	E	B	M	D
E	R	R	O	R
I	N	A	N	E
R	I	C	E	S
D	E	E	T	S

118

	T	O	F	U
S	H	R	U	G
A	R	I	N	G
N	E	O	N	S
D	E	N	Y	

119

A	G	E	S	
V	E	X	E	S
I	N	A	L	L
V	I	L	L	A
	E	T	S	Y

120

		A	B	A	R
D	E	N	A	L	I
A	R	C	H	E	S
M	O	H	A	V	E
	D	O	M	E	S
	E	R	A		

121

	R	A	W	
G	E	N	R	E
P	A	N	E	L
S	L	A	C	K
	M	L	K	

122

	S	L	O	W
C	H	I	N	A
U	R	B	A	N
L	U	R	I	D
T	B	A	R	

123

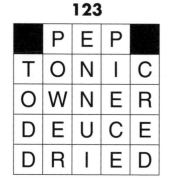

	P	E	P	
T	O	N	I	C
O	W	N	E	R
D	E	U	C	E
D	R	I	E	D

124

I	M	O	K		
T	A	P	I	R	
C	H	E	N	E	Y
H	A	N	G	D	O	G
	L	E	T	S	G	O
		D	U	E	I	N
			T	A	S	E

125

	W	A	R	M
		E	P	E	E
M	A	R	C	H
A	V	I	A	
Y	E	L	P	

126

	G	U	L	P
	U	H	O	H
P	L	A	I	D
S	L	U	R	
I	S	L	E	

127

	K	I	S	S
C	O	N	C	H
R	A	D	I	O
I	L	E	F	T
T	A	X	I	

128

		W	E	E
S	M	A	L	L
T	E	R	M	S
A	R	I	S	E
G	E	O		

129

P	L	O	T	
A	L	S	O	
R	O	C	K	Y
	Y	A	Y	A
	D	R	O	P

130

H	I	T		
E	R	U	P	T
C	A	B	L	E
K	N	E	E	S
		R	A	T

131

		S	A	D	
C	H	I	N	E	S	E
S	O	D	A	C	A	N
P	R	E		R	U	T
A	N	T	O	I	N	E
N	E	W	Y	E	A	R
		O	E	D	

132

	S	L	A	P
	T	O	R	T
F	A	C	T	S
I	R	K	S	
G	R	E	Y	

133

	D	R	E
A	S	I	A	N
V	I	V	I	D
I	R	O	N	S
S	I	T		

134

B	E	A	M	
A	R	M	Y	
G	R	U	M	P
	E	S	A	U
	D	E	N	T

135

	M	T	V	
R	E	H	A	B
E	L	U	D	E
C	O	M	E	T
	N	P	R	

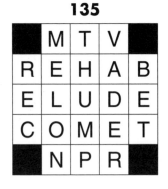

136

	A	D	A	M
T	W	I	C	E
A	G	A	I	N
N	E	R	D	S
K	E	Y	S	

137

	J	E	F	F
B	O	X	E	R
U	N	T	I	E
L	A	R	G	E
K	H	A	N	

138

A	S	P		H	O	P
D	I	E	T	E	R	S
O	R	E	I	L	L	Y
	L	L	A	M	A	
T	O	E	R	I	N	G
M	I	R	A	N	D	A
I	N	S		G	O	P

139

		H	E	R
B	R	A	D	Y
M	A	N	I	A
W	I	D	E	N
S	L	Y		

140

F	L	I	N	T
R	O	M	E	O
E	T	H	A	N
S	T	O	L	E
H	A	T	E	R

141

	A	P	P	S
I	D	E	A	L
R	A	T	I	O
A	G	I	N	G
N	E	T	S	

142

E	N	D	S	█
G	O	R	E	█
G	R	E	E	K
█	M	A	T	E
█	S	M	O	G

143

G	P	A	S	█
P	O	P	E	█
S	U	R	L	Y
█	R	O	M	E
█	S	N	A	P

144

█	P	A	D	S
L	A	P	U	P
U	P	P	E	R
N	E	L	L	Y
A	R	E	S	█

145

A	N	T		R	C	A
B	A	R	S	O	A	P
S	T	E	W	A	R	T
	H	E	A	D	S	
P	A	S	T	I	E	S
I	N	A	H	E	A	P
T	S	P		S	T	Y

146

	R	E	V	S
D	I	X	I	E
O	P	E	R	A
R	E	R	U	N
A	N	T	S	

147

S	A	M	S	
C	H	A	P	S
A	E	I	O	U
M	A	N	O	R
	D	E	K	E

148

	K	A	Y
S	M	O	R	E
H	E	A	R	T
O	S	L	O	
T	H	A	W	

149

R	E	S	T	S
A	C	U	R	A
M	O	D	E	L
P	L	A	N	E
S	E	N	D	S

150

	D	A	F	T
M	I	C	R	O
E	X	C	I	A
A	I	R	E	S
L	E	A	S	T

Looking for more Easy Crosswords?

The New York Times

The #1 Name in Crosswords

🏛 St. Martin's Griffin

Looking for more Hard Crosswords?

The New York Times

The #1 Name in Crosswords

St. Martin's Griffin

Looking for more Large-Print Crosswords?

The New York Times

The #1 Name in Crosswords

St. Martin's Griffin

Looking for more Sunday Crosswords?

The New York Times

The #1 Name in Crosswords

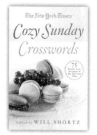

St. Martin's Griffin